Hams beneath the Firmament

Also by Terri Ford

Why the Ships are She
(2001)

Hams beneath the Firmament

poems by Terri Ford

Four Way Books
New York City

Distributed by
University Press of New England
Hanover and London

Please direct all inquiries to:

Editorial Office
Four Way Books
POB 535, Village Station
New York, NY 10014
www.fourwaybooks.com

Library of Congress Catalogue Card Number: 2006928240

ISBN: 978-1-884800-78-8

Cover art: Christian Schmit

Cover design: Cover design by Pablo A. Medina for Cubanica

This book is manufactured in the United States of America and printed on acid-free paper.

Four Way Books is a not-for-profit literary press. We are grateful for the assistance we receive from individual donors, public arts agencies, and private foundations.

This publication is made possible with public funds from the National Endowment for the Arts and from the New York State Council on the Arts, a state agency.

NATIONAL ENDOWMENT FOR THE ARTS

State of the Arts NYSCA

Distributed by University Press of New England
One Court Street, Lebanon, NH 03766

[clmp]
We are a proud member of the Council of Literary Magazines and Presses.

Acknowledgments

Miss Ford would like to thank the following publications where these poems first appeared:

Born Magazine: "Story Problem" first appeared in 2002 as an online collaboration with media artist Erik Loyer (http://www.bornmagazine.org/projects/storyproblem). This collaboration was later included in an interactive exhibit of *Born Magazine*'s ("Help Wanted," March 12-April 23, 2005) at the Center on Contemporary Art in Seattle, and was as well the subject of an interview in CIAC's *Electronic Magazine* (No. 17, 2003) with both Erik Loyer and me (http://www.ciac.ca/magazine/archives/no_17/en/entrevue1.htm).

The Cincinnati Review: "Dodo, 1974," "Gams beneath the Firmament," "Roger"

City Pages: "Dodo, 1974" first appeared in a cover story about poet laureates ("Wanted: Someone to Write an Ode to a Urinal," William Waltz, June 16, 2004, http://citypages.com/databank/25/1228/article12214.asp); for the story, five Minneapolis poets were challenged to write a poem about a Minnesota body of water.

Conduit: "Mister Hymen," "Waltzing at the Alcazar"

Forklift, Ohio: "Compelled," "Curfew at the Como Zoo," "In the rowboat of his dozing," "Story Problem," "The Sex Appeal of Spring," "Terri Ford Attempts a Ghazal," "Three Notes toward Thrush"

Incliner: "My Beautiful Horse Skirt"

Ploughshares: "Song for Two Bodies"

Steam: "Better Off"

"Bird Grandma" and "Aerial View of Me as a Premenstrual Bird" appeared in the anthology *What Light* (Minnesota Arts Organization and Magers & Quinn Booksellers, 2007).

I would also like to thank the Ohio Arts Council and the Fine Arts Work Center for a terrific summer in which I wrote many of these poems, and yes, the word "blue" does appear a disproportionate number of times. I want to thank Martha Rhodes, warmest editor, brilliant human bean; Eric, who lost a dedication but did inspire plenty; my family, my ever-lovin' family, who love me through each ruckus, cheer me on and hold me; Christian, who is a frickin' Genius; Matt, who could do a commercial for either crying or dancing; Margarine, for the nearness & the joy & the girl energy; Elizabeth, Bold Soul, Anne, my teachers and my tribe — sometimes they overlap to include the same people — and my widening circles, my public, my schools, to which I am true and in which I swim.

For Linda Dyer, my bold soul sister
(1961-2006)

Contents

1. The Jello of Elsewhere

Roger 3
Auto Shop Grandma 4
Dodo, 1974 5
Terri Ford Attempts a Ghazal 6
Psalm 7
Midwestern Livelihoods 8
In the rowboat of his dozing, Confucius wept. 9
Cancer Relay 10

2. The Fridge Door of Me

My Australia 13
My Life with Tarantino Subplots 14
One View of Gonorrhea 15
Mister Hymen 16
Hawk and Phlegm 17
Mine, in the Brush over Chester Creek 18
View of the Body Receding 19
Aerial View of Me as a Premenstrual Bird 20
Back Door Man 21
Death to the Budgie: A Public Service Announcement 22

3. Christ's New Clothes

Leeches: They were 25
Bird Ditty 26
My Life as the Song of the Ratite 27
Ian's Poem 28
My Boyfriend Is Calling, Hopped Up on Espresso 29

Curfew at the Como Zoo 30
The Blue Inside 31
What Her Body Thought 32
Big Night 33

4. How Green Was My Lunch

My Mother Stages the Resurrection 37
Waltzing at the Alcazar 38
My Beautiful Horse Skirt 39
What Budgies Think of in Heavy Traffic 40

5. Syncopated Bacon Birds

Before I Was Cool 43
Where the hell are the angels? 44
Women Standing in the Current 45
The Unaccountable 46
The Long Lunch of the Spirits 47
Better Off 48
Evensong 49
Greenhorn 50
Affirmations of the Body: Pennsylvania Turnpike 51
Budgie Jumpropes While Naming Names 52
Gams beneath the Firmament 53
Dr. Lavage Motors off at Dawn 54

6. My Baboon Heart

Haiku Budgie Style 57
Song for Two Bodies 58
The Association of Elvis with Spring 59
The Sex Appeal of Spring 60
Compelled 61
Star Walk 62
Three Notes toward Thrush 63
Whenever I kiss the dead, 64
Story Problem 65
Bird Grandma 66
Carrier Budgie 67
After my father left 68
About the Supply Closet, Floor 33 69
Rook in the Palm Tree 70

Notes 73

"I have tamed men of iron in my day,
shall I not easily crush these men of butter?"
—Ferdinand Alvarez de Toledo,
Duke of Alba (1508-82)

"The skilled audacity required to share an inner life"
—Gertrude Stein

"I am the woman powerful as a zoo."
—John Berryman,
from Dream Song No. 22, "Of 1826"

1

The Jello of Elsewhere

Roger

There's an army of men on the skywalk proceeding
each talking into the one hand held   to the ear. Roger. Ooh
I track the vital movements of soldiers in Dockers in Wranglers
in Sansabelt Polo and Levi. I heard one lie loud in line at the bank

who said unto his hand he was in some parking garage. All of them seem
to report location. Fie! Are they spies? Business casual boys
in cologne, the scent of them sinking me, Eau d'Anthrax...
Some of them in salt stained shoes staring down
in the elevator as though down there dwelt

the sorrow of sports. Some bear the man purse, bulgy
with task and sheaf. They walk the walk
of warlords. They are daily shavers. They nod valiant, call
each other chief.

Auto Shop Grandma

She is visored, bending, manic
on axels, rubs the universal
joints. Out
in the narthex Scotchtaping all
of the chrome back on: my Gram. She has no
second language, her lingo's the dangled
bulb caging wattage slung under hoods up O

the ache in the crook of her back   the wrench
in her hand   the hollered gorilla hydraulics
    the traffic inside.
So many gizmos, not one thing

quiverous.   I was born
of lubes and sparks and oiled
shadows dripping; mine the descent of coins
in the carseat   chinka clinking
richly down.

Dodo, 1974

Let us go in toto to Lake Dodo
where my sister crashed her pink Suzuki
and the raspberry vines grew dense and handsome.
My brother and I played Brain Transplant:
heads beneath the blinking lampshades of the goddess-armed
gooseneck, stuttered by light, until we said
like robots in turn, "I want
a dirtbike." "I want a poodle."
The lake's bottom was shift and silt.
My parents' marriage was almost over.
Raspberry pie, raspberry jam, the red
juice in our hair and fingers—

We weren't there long. Long enough
to drink contraband beer bought from the French Club,
long enough to mix sloe gin with Galliano
and learn the long kiss of my second cousin
on the long lawn down in the dark
to the dock. Watching Nixon's face
clenched on the screen of our far TV when he
resigned, the shock on the faces of
adulthood. The world was starting
to crack, an old mirror ghosted
in slivers. My father's red boat was pulled up
out of the lake and the dock dismantled. It was fall, the return
of acne, and I wore my hair in a shag.

Terri Ford Attempts a Ghazal

Rerun inside me, two faces go blue,
lit by the TV, its leak of slow blue.

If you swim with sharks, do not wear yellow.
I sing of Duane Slick and his elbows — blue —

Brain to the sofa, the carpet, house paint
Every impulse fired in my mom smoked blue.

I didn't know that they were my parents
watching them hollering through uh-oh blue.

My father, always told what to do, turned
volume on his life up radio blue.

Ringing the harbor, the houses are named:
Wisteria, Cosmos, bell that grows blue —

Why did they keep fighting through it so long?
The cold war, the sniped one, Jericho blew.

My sister, my brother, his car, her phone
I kept getting saved, God's undertow, blue . . .

My mother's embrace, her plea (I was mute).
Tilt her and fill her up medico blue.

Terri, the drowning are not yours to save.
The tentative stars. The name for low blue.

Psalm

The Lord is my Arctic, my tube
nosed bird. He hoppeth over
the surface of waters, my Jesus
bird who doth follow my ship.

He broods over cliff's edge, ponderous
over all of the penguins balancing
their eggs on their feet.

The Lord is my giant frigate bird. I am
his limpet, krill, and his plankton.
He is the blue and the ever
in waking, blue
in the wake.

Midwestern Livelihoods

The budgies of Owatonna drive tow trucks.
Budgies of Elko? Winos all.
The budgies of Swaledale: purveyors of
girdles. The budgies of Brule are cruel birds: guano
in hairdos just for spite.
The budgies of Hope, Minnesota fly over bodies
of water, wing up everlasting.

In the rowboat of his dozing, Confucius wept.

How tired he was of burning wise, of output, of
inscrutability, kissing   dry cheeks. They came

and came as they had unto Lincoln: their
implorings, the never-ending, the on

their knees. Confucius weep. He long
for the louche and the lorgnine, for

subversion, immersion in the jello
of elsewhere. He wants to turn

his hairless head from the fervent
girls, their poetry titles one just

can't keep straight. *If I stood*
in the rivering hammers. If I let go. If the dead

could fly. If I could O say how my shoes shone. If only.
If I sing the minnow and the minnow   holds still.

Cancer Relay

As long as there is music, the limited man will stand
in one place, dancing, on the grass, as we pass
laps on gravel. Some are stippled, antelopes
with dampened backs. One

tall woman, leonine, with Aztec earrings in a holstered
skirt; man in leather pants the color of mustard, making
devil's haste. I loll and chuff; I'm dropping pretzels

on the track. How pleased to sight
the marching band; they mill and finally
hoist their music, drums to sternum, clarinets

up. I like the trousers' ribboned
stripe, like the coiled braid at the shoulder;
beloved the plumey hats, stanching

wind. Later, most of them gyrating to the Bee Gees
and the Chicken Dance. Only a few band members left

in the stands, derisive. I would have been
with them, mutterous behind my hand. I would have left
my tuba pressing its wet ear to the grass.

2

The Fridge Door of Me

My Australia

Even the doctor says "down there." And going under —
he's in! in the tent between my knees, announcing like
some clean cave guide, "A pinch" or "Just a little

cold." The weather down there's *cold?* One ob-gyn
told me dimensions
of my cervix. How can I go on

like this? as though everyone in Perth sends bulletins
of Perth conditions, Perth import/export, humidity index, hats

of Perth. Makes me want to stand on the tour bus, point
and gawp, "Hey! Big Tom!" the way I did in London. Who

do I kid? Nobody gets to Perth anymore — it's too
darned far, the passage rough and long enough for three

life stories, maybe mine. Even now, the upstairs newlyweds
are banging bedposts and crying out, the rhythm

of the Perthian song.

My Life with Tarantino Subplots

Each morning the snowfall in the meth lab
window, that Candyland fence, one sex offender
who dwells above Subway, the barber school
of loud brothers outside: O my metro

transit fondest route. Each night the long shadow the stop sign makes
scares up a body beneath the tree. Each night I point out
to my hype hype self: it's a shadow. Dear. Some nights I feel
so far underwater I can't tell my hand

for my hand. *Why do you think*
you're so persistent? asks the man I keep asking
to say yes to me. Why? I shall not answer. For I am tired

of clues! Fuck microscopes, fuck footprints, fuck
the details crime comes in. Smooch my intuition, son, or
this mouthy mouth: smooch this. Lo what stale coffee

this station makes, what a small pair of glasses I carry
   outside   My God it's a body. Loop back. *His*
body? Ter, it's not any body.   I implore you, Director! can I

start over? This time in a Nancy Drew roadster, on a better
street, in the color of noon. This time
I wear a wire, entrap, entice, let the operatic sweet
strings start   and he says yes

One View of Gonorrhea

In the dream the beloved is raising his face to me
telling me he's seen everything. I mean he's seen
every guy in me, his germs, the sperm
in canoes. All this from the times he looked in
the fridge door of me, kept on

the light. In one version of the dream, he pats me
and says, "Ex-husband. Gonorrhea," and now I understand
he is leaving, but I am too busy counting asymptomatic
years (is this likely?) to notice, to ask him

please stay. In one version, he's not my boyfriend
just yet. We are teenagers out on the porch
not saying not saying goodnight. I just want

to kiss him, every cell in me allegiant
and then his mouth on my mouth,
the wind tunnel pulls us, I in my clothes
nearly sucked off me, he whose words
are thrown down south —

O words! when all we need
is mouth —

Mister Hymen

Relent, says he with his cigarillos, his
splintered windshield. You fain think
he's neat, is boss, is mustang,

yup. When he covers your north
with kisses,   oho the hymen
hies, bucolic   inland you're tossing

edelweiss, unmown and springing. This thump
and wag hath no repose   & when, how soon, he's

dying (says) — So you, as
foreordained, give   in. What he broke's
not glass, but a low grief, volcanic
and inactive years. See him run. All

of the villagers run
from heat, and you spread,
spread.

Hawk and Phlegm

Now is the season of hawk and phlegm,
when Garage Boy mounts his Litter Hawk
cruising all the levels of the parking
arcade, and I in my swaddling here
on Froome arise and rise: hawk hawk
pa tewwww. O lady of most human hawks, lean.

Lean over the sink as over ship's prow or
an ornament on some high-end hood and hark
and clear, hoy fist and spit. There. My

hankie. Thanks. On the ledge outside the
litigator's perch lived a lady hawk who hatched
her kind, who looked not
like much, maybe dark chicken dumb
on the nest, but in flight? Fierce

of talon, one scaring wingspan, beak
of the mighty mighty bird of prey. Stand
back. For she is macho and maketh her own

indelicate noise, barfing back her food
for her wee. Alert. Mess not
with us, neither shall you toy. We barf.
We hawk. We teach your kind.

Mine, in the Brush over Chester Creek

Rubber. Presser. Copper of first feels, his breathing
alarmed me — not to mention his mouth
of emergencies, over me, in the dark, in

the brush, yards away from our parents' windows: his mom
the local TV talk host, bright-eyed, coiffured, maybe
already drunk; my mom in her raucous

Jesus pants, leaning in to inhale
my probable Marlboro crimes. I wasn't afraid

of him, exactly; he was my brother's friend, and was at our house
the night I came in with my poodle dead in my arms.
He put his big shoes on the wrong feet
at the door, blurring, his head down,   crying too.

View of the Body Receding

When I begin to think that I've never seen him,
that I won't remember his shape coming nearer —
this is such silence, and in this silence, all
things lengthen — hemlines, workdays, the shadows
hills move into, lists. And we

won't meet. He'll never
kiss me.   And this grieves me so

that I'm not here   the husk of me passing
across the square   the way the wild-eyed speak

of the rapture.

Aerial View of Me as a Premenstrual Bird

A thing, a red thing, a thing that is red
with a tomahawk head   stomping or tilting,
will give up, is crying   on anthills   on eggshells

and O are there words   and birds for them, perched
on the hot wires suspended   and this red bird who
listens   hears only the words down

to gauging the pure sad   Bird takes a mood.
If Bird could sing today above flugelhorn,
she would focus on the sins   of others. Bird is

a sadness, a vigor, activity   burgeoning outward
& this day is magnified   7 x 7 x 7 x

Bird   she remembers
stays in the chimney all night
nervous & napping hard, beak
under wing.

Back Door Man

Okay, times I miss him who used the word titty
who knew the whole forest, lunarscape, pittance
of me   who located flood plains and causeth all
the tiddlywink trees to convulsively wink. Who entered
me like a clown in a cannon and gave me deep sleep.

For other times (now) I remember how he didn't listen, how little
he knew me, he who asked questions like had I seen that car show?
and how when he did reveal, I listened to him as though I were bleeding.
And all of the estuaries got real mad. And all of the tiddlywink trees
throughout the bacterial causeway became like unto
the apple orchard of ire in the witch's forest, shouting out ow
and muttering vile at the passers by.

Death to the Budgie: A Public Service Announcement

There's a menace wields a skillet: Teflon is the silent killer.
The budgie life is a life of PERIL. Beware of anything on this list:
burning candles, scented candles, plug-in air fresheners (deadly oil
that seeps), air conditioners, drafts, monsoons. If you deign let
your budgie out: ceiling fan blades, dastard children (high pitch, sudden
moves), halogen lamps (death by flame), doors in motion, bathtubs, sinks
& toilets. Enjoy your budgie. Keep him safe
from the proverbial glass full or half (he could drown!!),
bookshelves budgie could fall behind, electric cords, your goddamned

feet, dogs, cats, yarn, open windows, and of course the drunk
with her tiny window of judgment, opening cage doors on a lark.

3

Christ's New Clothes

Leeches. They were

undulating, then dulating. The cadence
of scuba. Evening stockings. Icking licorice
lilty fingers, seeking to adhere to kiddie ankles,
tummies, limbs. BLOODSUCKERS, we'd shriek and peel them
off in sheer Dread, pour on them towers

of Morton Salt. Oh, they'd shrivel down sure
foreshortened and shriven, as a witch to her hat   and Die
Sucker Die on the dock on the
shore on the rocks by the lawnchairs shrubs the

grave of my poodle. What a fierce
dominion, barefoot over a gang
of black thumbs, suckless

and beached. We shook salt and hummed
like the righteous. Dingalings. Cousins.
Kids.

Bird Ditty

I have not been a bird for years. But if I go back
I'll be the be-bop bobolink in Amherst — Emily's
chump of a speed bump canary. The bohunk belle
lifts her feathered skirts, and pogo queen, she bounces
boing diddy boing to the graveyard ravens, to the
stuffed ravens in the airport gift shop, flapping
their yaps off to Baltimore.

My Life as the Song of the Ratite

My emu came from Greenville.
I sent my emu to Ino, Wisconsin,
to work his herky-
jerky hoodoo. Flightless

the emu, blue   is his throat. Shaglike
the hairdo crowning my emu; her emlets
like islets or zyglots   behind —

Nomadic my emu like the shamans
of yore; when he runs he sways
as though running were effortless
effortless joy. My emu in fact

is the chief of his village, master
over unincorporated Ino; proportionately
like being the king of cubic zirconium,

but shhhh then, the emu doesn't
know. He sounds like a shaman, the wild
drumlike sound from his throat, but runs
like a girl, bouncy for arrhythm, tufty

the hair that covers his mind,
my emu sprockets toward Port Wing, toward
Bayfield, flightless my emu, fightless

his eye, fierce in his voice out, blue
is his throat.

Ian's Poem

Ian eccentric beyond belief. Ian onstage dragging talk
like a pool repairman speaking dolphin, a Texan
spaceman talking sex. Ian come in from the out of doors in his

bubble coat and his somebody's
brother cowlick hair, who crossed
to me in that mesmerized way I finally see as a guy's

being taken. So take me. He's telling me now of the open fields
in his music, free space; I'm being perplexed — I don't see
how to listen (& picture Julie Andrews running) — when Ian
emits a sound and walks away in the lope

of his beer. Ian, do not belch in my poem. It was going to be
a storm and blow back poem: back to the part where you smiled
and took my hand and said, "That was good. I'm Ian."

My Boyfriend Is Calling, Hopped Up on Espresso

If ever two lichens likened unto
their liebchens, we are such

lichens. If ever the mollusks
would polish their bottoms, we could

like them more. And if just once the blind
ghost pilot knife fish could shake down
the shark tank, if I can stand still

while the manta ray in its fluid poncho the color
of latte swims over me thrice, then you will take
a breath and allow me

to speak, and I won't confuse you
with my mother not hearing,
and I can put this on a separate floor
of my head from the ex-husband shouting,

and you will know I am not your father
chasing you with a hammer
for the crime of looking just

like him. If you lower your voice, you can hear my whisper
in the least seahorse looping its tail to its home
fern. Honey, hi.
It's me.

Curfew at the Como Zoo

After all of the people leave, the lowland
gorillas stop rushing the glass in the monkey house.
They don't lob fistfuls of rock or lawn overhand
at the gauche lookers-on lolling

up there. It is their silence, earned. It's dusk, and the
orphaned mountain lions stop their pacing, which is
public pacing: actually they like this place; they find

in the zoo their own Fat City. The snow leopard
quits with the nervous aerobic leaps; when the humans
go, he puts on some Coltrane and starts

to dance. The flamingos practice
a new stance; the lemurs open beers
and begin to imitate the mom who kept saying, "See
the lemur? That's a lemur," as though children

were idiots. Only the polar bear has to continue his swim hysteric
in the same hundred circles, surfacing at the permitted loop, over, just
a thousand times more and he'll turn in. And the wolves

can't stop what they do when they have
to do what they do: they howl back
at the sirens; they lean back their throats
and give themselves over to crying an answer, if there could be
an answer   to the blue world over.

The Blue Inside

Not the blue of spruce, not the grievous
fathom blue of lakes, not turpentine. The blue

inside the Zoloft bottle is a calming blue,
like a drowned sky floating in Christ's

new clothes. Not the slow stars swarming
on your dark screen, not the shade of the slow
Corolla you drive behind, not a brazen blue

like the color that his eyes would be, if his eyes
would be, if he saw, if he — A wash, just the thought

of blue; later you could never be certain
of what you'd made up: oh, this

is your story. Chinamen's blue, the spooked blue
of the future. Blue of bereft, the hound's
long song on the porching dusk, or Arctic sharp
your ache for the loss
of him.

What Her Body Thought

Her body thought it would break
the glass beakers and never
dissolve. When he asked, her body
thought that he tasted like drums, like

a theorem, a dial tone, bagpipes,
the roof. Thought

that he was convection and she
was the stovetop replying
in rings. Her body found itself
overloud, public the way

that the mangoes are public. Her body
thought of the dark as a thigh, as
inland, the skateboarder blaring home
on the asphalt. Her body thought

that the weather was oatmeal, that she
could not rise. Her body knew
there were sorrows stored in it the size
of a speedboat. She drove them out

and then slept in the boathouse
and breathed.

Big Night

It was in the arctic or in
the desert when Jesus' enemies came
for him and the bigshot disciple
cut off the ear of one

of the henchmen. *Weren't you*
with him? said one of the guys around
a fire, but Peter at the party
said, *I'm not your man* and shrugged, and when

he got another chance to be
a stand-up man, again
with the *No*, and a third
time, the connection he fought, he said

(louder) *No, I don't*
know him. And I
know Peter, I might have lain
with Peter, misguided, up
all night, thoroughly seen
and loved anyway: guy
in the riot gear, in a cape, in

a heap, in his north
face parka, sobbing his stupid
sodden human

sounds, and the rooster
sound, and the two-way radio
dead and severed, the mountain
gone cold.

4

How Green Was My Lunch

My Mother Stages the Resurrection

The minister of the Methodist Church
off 35E is gasping a little, dragging

thrones. All the foiled lilies arranged
kittywompus to look like

a garden, except that she adds garden gloves (was plastic
invented before the first Easter?) and a fine
and shining garden spade. We all approve

of the trampled bedsheets, ripped sunder
and side. Judas' money bag
I am less sure of — it looks to be suede and from Neiman's
markdown — and are those not pesos? strewn from it
in an over-intended

cascade — I know, I know. My mother tries. She will recount
to me later how the Nelsons admired it, how much the Campbells

exclaimed. Worthy, unworthy. She keeps knocking on me
like the lit picture of Jesus, poised to enter

a clean home past dusk. My door
is dark here and I
don't rise.

Waltzing at the Alcazar

Alcazar Hotel
Cleveland Heights, Ohio

Off of the ballroom, we looked in the
storerooms, the Strange wading
through chairs to pet a black desk; we pointed

— the cardboard Indian scout who pointed
through the window's grime: Elizabeth knelt
at the waffle iron as though over a dying
soldier and cried out, *Crumbs! Oh, talk*

to me!   — Astonished
by Donoghue, putting down his coffee cup
in the ballroom, opening his arms

for a waltz. Which poets don't know
how to do anymore, and crashed & counted
  bumped   the dodge and burn —

So we looked out the window, excusing
ourselves to the ghosts of the waltzers
who met at the tea dance. *See how that street* (just
that band of it, between the full trees),

it looks so mysterious from here, but isn't.
I travel that street, he tells me. How the lives

of others appear to us. How we trip in the ballroom,
eminent, dancing. I think of this later, reading
in the courtyard a war survivor's diary — a woman
received a card from the front in her son's
handwriting: *I am still alive, I am still*
alive, I am still alive. And Elizabeth, walking
through the screen.

My Beautiful Horse Skirt

Horsie wendeth on the warp of the flannel of my horsie
skirt. I am a landscape hip to hip and mostly resemble
the innermost of a sleeping bag, Cheyenne, '63. Here

is the noble horse in profile, here's the flannel panel snugs
the zip. O horsing nostrils: soft shall you snuffle beyond

my knees. Lead a horse to, straight from the noun-here's mouth:
discard. My horse leads me. Still waters, sad eyes, cumulus &

black bra black bra black bra.

What Budgies Think of in Heavy Traffic

with contributions from John I. Lahti and Daisy Fried

How green was my lunch!
How dactylic my teensy steps
How fant is my bouf
How feng was my shui

How mystic my tan
How wack was my intergalactic
How gee was my budge

How chuck was my woody
How fast are those falcons
How wide were my wings
How loud can I sing
How long parakeet   not long   enough

5

Syncopated Bacon Birds

Before I Was Cool

I poked voodoo pinholes through the brown eyes
of Rolf Huff, through the eyes
of Julie Buck, through the eyes
of my best friend Stanley, through the eyes
of everyone in the second grade. Except for mine eyes scrunched
into my school camera grin. There, in the Brownie uniform
buttoned so wrong I hunched the top row happy.

Before I was cool I would sing anything
out loud, I believed in twins who were spies. Before I was cool
I was most absorbent. A bridesmaid in seven series of wrong
wrong shrine. You could burn me. Anyone

could. When I was cool, I turned
to liquids, a slur brooking
to snow. A widening changeable
thaw. Am I loud

enough? Who's that
through the pinhole? Whose
narrow voice is it what sings?

Where the hell are the angels?

Might could be they're bending over sinks in their
brassieres, giving one another perms. Might be lighting

ciggies end to end, interrupting each other, talking
of lesser Theys: arch cardinals, lesser
wingspans, snow. Couldn't they stop

with their cackle and nattering? Whose job is it
to singe, to halt my friend's tumor? Do they not

see me here? Where the fuck are they?
I'm going to bang on this bell til they come.

Women Standing in the Current

My cabdriver Charlie's explaining how gravity has all the properties
of a current you can't swim   against. I think of the
persuasive stream. Then I remember last Monday,
how all across the Eastern seaboard

women I know were hauling back their arms with hammers, poised
to smash shells or glass or for all I know Volkswagens, which means to us
we disperse Linda's cancer to the ends of the sea. Almost 10 a.m. and her

surgeon lathers, they pull white drapes, someone holds for the doctor
a gown. The daughter of the marine biologist
has got shells and a sidewalk and a
ballpeen hammer: oh how   she razes, with all the length of her stroke
she hefts. Ann Scott, in the city, brings out

on the asphalt the shells she has collected for years.
She must alarm pedestrians,
resolute, to smithereens.
Lauren's home late and to the backyard, bashing,
all her might — bang scrape against   cement. And my god,

Cammy! in a circular
dust mask, like a surgeon in drag,
she's pulverizing an entire bathroom,
sink and toilet, disintegration, stone, to

bits. I'm just running errands, it's the last day my car works and also
my blowdryer dies. All the power in the great house dims.
It's the last day of Linda's left breast.

The Unaccountable

And the snow kept falling, snow for pounds, snow like pounds
of flowers   fell   fell for the infirm, fell on
the yelpers, fell in with war buds   fell for the lovesick, fell
through the birdprints that dither the shore

The snow fell all night in fistfuls without any noise. Shut up
the glass flowers   UP
I want my mom back, is what my friend said. And I don't even
touch his face.

The Long Lunch of the Spirits

Sometimes I fear we will use up
the vowels, O the mad plans
of the body joicing,   rejoicing. Meantime
our spirits are out eating lunch   and still eating, still

telling anecdotes, weeks later, spreading joyous gestures
over orange peels and water glasses, banging cutlery

with laughter, for emphasis, and sometimes we lean near, look
into each other, murmurous   almost
   like   song   and I think saying something

in favor of samba or one
hundred plans in the rush   lovers do.
And in none of this

is there yearning; it is all answer, all coming, all came,
though the body's been hiding beneath the table,

its knees drawn up, its wide face down,
where no one would see it was crying
for all it could not believe in and never
ever expected   to keep.

Better Off

When I let him go, I will rise from the earth
and be borne up, balloon
my shoes, balloon
my tooth, balloon

haiku. When resentment lifts, fireflies
shall alight in my skirt and beep with me, high over
the lawn and the globular
peonies, this aggressive

riffing air. When the yearning
stops, if it ever stops, I will dance

the most strenuous hula, and mine own
cabana boys will candle me back down, signal

the all-clear, and I will
come home, safely in slow mo
drifting on down.

Evensong

When you are tired   as
  a heavy tulip   drowsing
when   you   cannot   keep   up

after a night of babbling, dancing, arm-wrestling
bull ridin' with one arm up   high and blind
and your hoo-ha whiskey birthday friend grins
and your radiant friend, ginger with the knee
injured hopping naked over a campfire, and
the whiskey shags with the radiant,
dips her

when your friends trail home, slow and reluctant
and you are still home in the last waftings of their good

nights: remember your brother
how his former wife threatened to sneak in his bed
and cut off his hair & the many nights of fear
obstacle   secret   remember

his honeymoon   her scream & scream
  the police   :   when you
 are safe   when you sleep

nights through   watched over   Jesus
 Mary Joseph   it's dark

Greenhorn

Here is my hand in travel toward Man
Toward Man extended my hand on pause
Mattering singled out dumb shucks

Oh try   And here are the night leaves
ashimmer in rain holes   Here are the small birds
rinsing their feet   Look there: the tulips & white nuns

we're swaying   The kiwis the toucans the plumage
which breathes   My throat is humming the night

full of hammers   Dog song and creme rinse
My hat's in my hand.

Affirmations of the Body: Pennsylvania Turnpike

I will drive through the pages of my Triptik.
I will not press barbells on my sparkly weightbench
beside my rig in full view on road's shoulder. Will

not. I will watch the weasel shimmy
into the grasses. When I drive through the tunnel at Kittatinny
Mountain, I shall not dwell on the Paris
tunnel, its tiles, the crumpled

car   nor the many many bodies
of deer   gutted, bloated, dragged near

the gulley: by who? And the multitudinous ruffs
of the tire treads at roadside: how
do they get there? And the plastic bags

in rags in the trees... And when the moon
turns the one eye of its face
on me, like the face
of Robert Creeley, smiling; like
the undocumented side of the Lyle
Lovett face, like the Power Ranger face

of my love: let the furnace blast, let the force
of its light lift me up, be all I ever hope
to bear.

Budgie Jumpropes While Naming Names

Budgie at the precinct. Budge knows Jack.
Bell with a hard-on. Twelve-bird Bob.
Teen of the long tonsil. L. Jail Bait.
Glockamorra cockamamie half-baked Jake.
Syncopated bacon birds all underwired
Louie on the fibrillator
Salo on the shore
Budgie li'l stool pigeon scores four more.

Gams beneath the Firmament

I'd been summoned under stars
by Dr. Lavage and his goldfinch Diffley.
Hungered my bodice Dr. Lavage
(at least by half) & we slept on his deck
but be low brow   oh the undone down   damn he was cozy,

pale without his specs, blinking up
into the firmament asking which one's Orion.
Had he the smooth moves of ten greased men,
I still could not name stars or saints.

And Diffley drowsed
while everything urgent beneath orbits
surged —   Til dawn the saga of Lavage.
Gifted we slept under the wild and inkity blue.

Dr. Lavage Motors off at Dawn

Much too early the doctor arises
to motor to the St. of Cloud. Doth beam, barefooting —
even in autumn Lavage is shoeless —
and yet disapproves of the snap in the air.

But the stars! Dr. Lavage leans back his throat to them and,
spectacled this time, points out Orion,
which I know but don't say at this blue cloudless hour
is Orion's sanitary belt. Humid the mouth of my love
in his smooch at my gate —

Pad I back to the homestead
gently farting in my flannel gown

6

My Baboon Heart

Haiku Budgie Style

The budgies of Clear Lake are free and braless.
They carry a trill in the hooks of their beaks.
Oh say can't you hear   the autoharp strum?

Song for Two Bodies

Lumber me up, my licky bloke,
my one so far unseen, my limbered
timber boy. What luck

to bucky suck til sated,
luminous tuneful body
to play on, even now long play

me on. I hanker for
the slow bang of my love,
his howl and cheek, shebang, the flaming

oh's of his moany
mouth. There will be tongues,
I think, and bells.

The Association of Elvis with Spring

When tulips begin deployment
When midget pink bikes obfuscate driveways
When every stamen to its pistol starts
its drilling, loll and smear —
Then Elvis emerges from the army
and females everywhere
fall back to earth.

When the bellbottoms start to chime,
When the rakes down the lane
 uncover new rock,
When the nurseries assemble
 their green noisome upstarts,
Then you better gyrate, honey, work
 those hips.

And your thoughts turn to Graceland, its
27 televisions, TCB with a lightning
bolt, jungle room deluxe, Elvis sputting
on his golf cart. You recall a woman

on TV near his grave saying into
the camera how the death of Elvis
meant more to her than the deaths

of those her nearest
kin. Are you kin? You're thinking
how you'd appear in white, with
sideburns, crooning. Sweet grass toothes,
noodles up
through the earth.

The Sex Appeal of Spring

So spring slangs in with its disinformation —
dissing all the sissy mittens, whiffling
the attentively static hairdos

of March. March, the month
of cauterizing blizzards: may all the girls
go stumping home in their salt-stained shoes. Stupid

winter, still slinging hash, a sinkful
of ex-spouse, whisker trimmings, slur
and paunch... Or fiendish bright, still
snow, abashing us, sounding off

the roof in blobs, in whoosh and plurrups.
April, can you mean what you blurt, limning
every cruellest branch with your blowsy light, tarting up
the yards with daffs, runnelling down
the stone lane toward nuns? O which star

can I fix on now? I got need
to be fixed. Spring, you minx, let your stunt
sounds rip. Let the ice break up
on the lake, may every stalk like magic rise
and beefcake Jesus move that stone.

Compelled

Terri Ford, you are brilliant. You don't
go to sleep and you don't; you keep
on, your boot stepping oomph into the boat

of the body, the helmsgirl
has to play Solitaire til she wins. What is wrong
with you? I say, Shut up; the siblings in me

take their swipes, and I am the machine
going on, sometimes hours. Why won't the cards

fall in their order, the right one
I ordered? black Jack on the
Queen of the red pinhole
of my heart — Terri Ford, fucked, on
the pinions of glory, go
home.

Star Walk

This is one for Kosmos' brother
who in his mind was gliding

over the earth, who to his mother
was trampling the garden, bobbling slow
in his astronaut boots, who to his brothers

was clinically insane, tethered, dragging
the hairdryer hose affixed to his helmet
when they watched from inside the lit house,
gasping, doubled over, spitting and weeping

with laughter. This is for the youngest brother
who meant to do something first
and mankind-size, who was so encumbered stepping

off of the porch into pumpkin vines, who saw
himself soaring on some other edge,
lighter, breathing the upper air
in which he would be recognized.

Three Notes toward Thrush

One of my friends is a transistor monkey.
One of my friends is an open-mouthed bird.
One of my chairs is piled high with black clothes.
One night I ended in nine bars of noise.

On New Year's Day, I heard the bay hounding.
On your conscience may the hoon ray furl.
On Maddy's blue wrist, you can trace a home world.

O the baby sleeping like a boneless hot cookie.
O to lose my heading in the high horse way.
O the sudsing in me when you love up my name-o.
To end the last time on a clear glass note.

Whenever I kiss the dead,

the deepest snowbank in all the Dakotas
sobs a little, connecting to the Red River
flowing the other way   I can't go.

When I use my voice for naming my dead,
everything under the lawn feels urgent
up to its throat.

When they close the box and take up
the shovels, when the hymnals
shut, when my tears fall onto

the dead: it's because of the river
of letting go, how the dead let go
        when they go   where they go —

Is the river empty? Will it empty for me?

Story Problem

Three heads have I in Oh-hi-oh.
In Ohio three red heads have I.
If I want and need one head, yet I am of two minds,
what color is my bike, and when can I wheel home
over the smashed petals yards from the sea?

Three rinsed bras drip in the shower.
In my shower, six blue cups drip.
Are there 3 separate tunes? And how many stormfronts
will pass through, subside? Who would my friend be
if she was not broken?

If it's three a.m. in my white room,
in my room (I'm white), say it's three —
and I phone my arbitrage broker in Tokyo —
what time is it when the school dance ends?
How many will walk home dejected as gypsum?
What's the proportion to Giddyfoot there, hardly
dampening lawns? When does the longing end,
if it ends? What's the name of that blue?

Bird Grandma

If a bird sang itself full of rainwater and tried to breathe through
that lake: that's how she sounds. And the night in her mouth raspy
and open, discontinuous. One blue eye
opens too when you touch her arm and speak or lightly stroke
her forehead. She used to lie on the beach
in her tropical skirted two-piece swimsuit
with plastic DQ spoons on her eyelids.
She doesn't eat or talk or know
it's spring the way a deaf woman doesn't know that birds
make sound. There's a lake inside her rising up her ragged lungs;
its dark will drown her inch by inch.

Carrier Budgie

Done gone rode down the elevator with
the body of Gram. Say
that's not a metaphor, bird. Bring forth
her choppers, her silver
dollars, my dipstick, meds. Fetch me
my black shoes, hie we

to the chapel for there may be many weddings but only
the one funeral, budge, you dig? As for lately,

I'm standing here on the Astroturf holding the heft
of a box full of once-Gram. Somebody says
the clouds resemble a bathing suit. When the budgie
calls, I think it's a loon, lonesome   over the lake in the budgie
airspace

After my father left

we wanted a snapshot, just us, & clean
(& some of us older, & some of us
thinner), we posed. I still

have the best shot — my mother & sister
in gales so hard their eyes blew shut,
my brother with his mouth

wide open, holding his belly; my head
turned to look up, my face is
a guess — my family sounding
without sound, laughing and dying with tears
out the sockets, relieved
as we will ever be.

About the Supply Closet, Floor 33

A box of them abide in there:
in the shadows on the shelves —
the latex examination gloves.
They say the gloves are there in case
one fears the anthrax, fears the mail —
But I know why. For my baboon heart.

Last week at the allergist's
another patient walked toward my socks
patterned with cow brown spots
& exclaimed, "Oh! I thought
your ankles were bleeding!" O ask not why
the gloves are kept on 33. Because
of my ankle stigmata.

Once I was afraid of the cloakroom,
idiot mittens hung in the damp in
the dank in the dank dark clink. Once my troubles
were merely shallow breathing & heights.
Don't even speak about those gloves. Jesus
could come any minute to reach in
as though through a drive-up window. He wants to hold
(like Lennie his bunny) my baboon heart. I swan.
I say. Put it back now. Christ.

Oh, and when I said allergist's? I meant:
camp. When I said cloakroom, it was
code for: condo. When I say supply closet
I so mean the live stove of my body. Anyone
could just reach in. My wee chimping
cardio. My simpering valves. My compromised half my left
made right. Draw on the latex. Open
that door.

Rook in the Palm Tree

My neck is the stem of the oldest palm tree
in Hollywood Hills. My wings are hinges
to library doors where you come to read all that the mouth

can't say. My mouth? The flapjack jabberwocky perched
in yonder pine. In my kneecaps I keep
the secret tongues of the racehorses
gasping, pell-mell. In my hair reside haircuts I haven't
yet met. My belly the red red yaw of the turtle, its mandible

jaw. My populous forehead: blazing women in nightgowns breaking
in the wide river of sound. In my back are lodged the game pieces
I've swallowed: rook in the palm tree, queen
on the wing, the silver Monopoly boot ballchanging

on my spine. My clavicle is the autoharp longing
for teacher to come pick me up. My ankles

are the men on the roof with the chainsaws. When I rise, my feet
are rowboats containing a total of 66 kings. All of them
are blackened timber. All of them
are standing upright.

NOTES

"Bird Ditty" was composed of alternate lines by the avid birder Robert Ayres and the never birder Miss Ford.

Terri Ford's first book of poems, *Why the Ships Are She,* was published by Four Way Books in 2001. A fellow at the Bread Loaf Writers' Conference, Miss Ford was also profiled in June of 2004 in the Minneapolis newspaper *City Pages* as one of five Minnesota poets who might be the state poet laureate if Minnesota had one. Most recently, her poems have appeared in *Agni, Cincinnati Review, Conduit, Forklift Ohio,* and *Ploughshares,* among others, as well as in the anthology *Poetry Daily: The Best from the World's Most Popular Poetry Website* (Sourcebooks, 2003). She has received fellowships from the Kentucky State Arts Council, the Kentucky Foundation for Women, and the Ohio State Arts Council. She currently lives in Minneapolis, where she hopes to change at least the lipstick on the face of Minnesota poetry.